ANIMAL SOS!

SAVE THE HUMPBACK WHALE

WINDMILL BOOKS
New York

Published in 2014 by Windmill Books, An Imprint of Rosen Publishing
29 East 21st Street, New York, NY 10010

Produced for Windmill by Calcium Creative Ltd
Editors for Calcium Creative Ltd: Sarah Eason and Rachel Blount
US Editor: Joshua Shadowens
Designer: Emma DeBanks

Photo   credits: Cover: Shutterstock: Melissaf84.
Inside: Dreamstime: Abarreras 23, Adeliepenguin 14, Captblack76 22,
Flukeprint 6, Guynamedjames 24, Outdoorsman 6–7, Yuvis 1;
Shutterstock: 9, Aquapix 20, BioLife Pics 8, BMJ 21, Ethan Daniels 18, James
Michael Dorsey 13, Karel Gallas 5, Patricia Hofmeester 15, Gertjan Hooijer
12, Stanislav Komogorov 19, Jan Kratochvila 25, Jay Ondreicka 29,
Ami Parikh 27, Photoman29 4, Siraphat 16, Bjorn Stefanson 10,
Albert H. Teich 26, John Tunney 17, Wdeon 11, Paul S. Wolf 28–29.

Library of Congress Cataloging-in-Publication Data

Spilsbury, Louise.
Save the humpback whale / by Louise Spilsbury.
pages cm. — (Animal SOS!)
Includes index.
ISBN 978-1-4777-6041-3 (library) — ISBN 978-1-4777-6034-5 (pbk.) —
ISBN 978-1-4777-6045-1 (6-pack)
1. Humpback whale—Juvenile literature. 2. Endangered species—Juvenile
literature. I. Title.
QL737.C424.S724 2014
599.5'25—dc23
                                        2013027009

Manufactured in the United States of America

CPSIA Compliance Information: Batch #BW14WM: For Further Information contact Windmill Books, New York, New York at 1-866-478-0556

Contents

Humpback Whales in Danger

Humpback whales are truly magnificent wild animals. These sea **mammals** weigh an average of 66,000 pounds (30 t) and can grow as long as a school bus. Unfortunately, their mighty size and weight are not enough to save them from dangers caused by people.

A Humped Back

The humpback whale is named for the way the small **fin** on its back sits on a hump, which you can see when the whale arches its back to dive. Another way to tell the humpback from other whales is by its very long, narrow **flippers**. These can be one-third of the whale's entire body length.

The humpback is one of the most acrobatic whales.

Humpback Whale Losses

Into the twentieth century, people hunted so many humpback whales that they reduced the number to around 10 percent of the original population. Today, there are only around 60,000 humpback whales. These remaining whales are still at risk and need to be protected from dangers.

Humpback whales dive head-first.

Rescue the HUMPBACK WHALE!

Be informed. Find out all you can about humpback whales, and talk to other people about these magnificent animals. Reading this book is a good way to start.

Humpback Whales in the Wild

Humpback whales are found in all oceans of the world, but they do not stay in one place. Every year, humpback whales **migrate**. They swim from warm waters to cold waters, and back again!

On the Move

In the summer, humpback whales live in cool waters near the poles, where they feed on fish and tiny animals called **zooplankton**. In the winter, they swim to warmer waters closer to the **equator**, where they give birth to their young. Some humpback whales make a round trip journey of 10,000 miles (16,100 km) in one year!

Humpback whales travel to warmer waters to give birth to babies.

6

Diving for Food

Humpbacks are **baleen** whales. Most baleen whales migrate in different seasons. Baleen whales have no teeth. Instead, they have baleen plates. These are bristly, comblike parts in the whales' mouths that they use like filters. The whales feed by swallowing large mouthfuls of water and filtering food out of the water with the baleen.

Humpback whales travel to cold waters to feed.

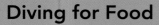

ANIMAL SOS

Humpback whales in Oceania, and a small, isolated population in the Arabian Sea, are in serious danger of becoming **extinct**.

7

Humpback Whales' Biggest Enemy

The humpback whale does have animal enemies. The whale's natural **predators** include orcas and large, fierce sharks, such as tiger sharks or great white sharks.

Fast Exit

Humpbacks escape many predators because they travel in groups called pods. There is safety in numbers because there are more whales to spot danger. Humpbacks are also powerful swimmers. They use their massive tail fin, called a fluke, to propel themselves through the water. They also use the fluke to push themselves right out of the water, landing with a tremendous splash!

Humpback whales usually swim and feed as a group.

Human Hunters

Humpbacks are powerful swimmers, so the predators that hunt them usually catch only sick, weak, or young whales. Many humpback flukes bear the scars of unsuccessful attacks. The whales' main enemy is people. Humpbacks swim mainly near coasts and migrate to the same regions each year, so people have been able to easily find them and hunt them down.

Great white sharks follow and attack humpback whales.

ANIMAL SOS!

Between 1905 and 1983, an estimated 200,000 humpback whales were killed by people in the southern **hemisphere** alone!

Hunted!

From the seventeenth to the early twentieth centuries, people hunted humpback whales for their **blubber**, meat, and bones. People ate whale meat, and boiled blubber to extract oil to burn in lamps and to use in soap. They also made buttons and other items from the whales' bones.

Hunting Today

Today, large-scale whaling in most countries is banned. Some **indigenous** hunters catch humpback whales, but only in small numbers and to feed their families. However, some countries still hunt whales. They say that they catch these amazing creatures to study them, but whale meat is sometimes found for sale in restaurants.

This was a busy whaling village before whale hunting was banned.

Whale Blubber

A humpback whale's blubber helps the animal survive. The blubber is a thick layer of fat under the whale's skin. It can be up to 20 inches (50 cm) thick. The fat stops the whale from becoming cold while it feeds in polar waters. It also gives the whale **buoyancy**. This helps the animal to float in the same way that a rubber ring helps people float.

This ship is used for hunting whales.

Rescue the HUMPBACK WHALE!

In 1946, the International Whaling Commission (IWC) was set up to control the whaling industry. It made rules about hunting certain whales, and banned hunting in areas where whale numbers were in decline. It also set hunting seasons to stop whales from being killed during breeding.

Dangers of Drowning

Whales are not fish that can breathe underwater. Like people, they are mammals, and must come to the surface to breathe air. If they cannot reach the surface to breathe, they drown.

Trapped in Nets

Humans pose a serious threat to humpbacks and other whales when they carry out certain types of fishing. In drift net fishing, huge nets are left to drift in the open ocean. If a whale becomes caught in a net, it panics, thrashes around, and gets tangled in the net. The trapped whale cannot swim to the surface for air and drowns.

Nets from large fishing ships can kill humpbacks.

Breathing with Blowholes

A whale can hold its breath for a long time, so it can swim to great depths. When it surfaces, it breathes through its **blowhole**. A blowhole is a hole in the skin that is covered by a flap. The flap stops water getting into the blowhole when the whale is underwater. At the surface, the whale opens its blowhole, lets out stale air, and then breathes in fresh air.

Humpback whales, like all baleen whales, have two blowholes on their heads.

Rescue the HUMPBACK WHALE!

Find out if your school lunch helps whales. Was your canned fish caught by methods that do not harm whales and dolphins?

Collisions

Humpback whales live along coasts. They sometimes swim close to shore, and even into harbors and rivers. They also give birth to and feed their young close to shore. There, they are at risk of being hit by passing boats.

Fatal Impacts

Thousands of whales die every year when they collide with passing boats. If a whale is hit by a heavy boat or its propeller blades, the injuries can be fatal. In areas that have a lot of boat traffic, whales may be frightened away and move to new areas that do not have as much food.

Boats can accidentally hit humpbacks that swim close to land.

Sleeping Beauty

Some whales are hit while they are resting. Whales rest near the ocean surface, while floating in the water. They must wake up regularly, to breathe. Scientists believe that humpback whales sleep by shutting down one half of their brain. The side that is awake remembers to surface and breathe.

Humpback whales can nap while they are on the move!

ANIMAL SOS!

In Glacier Bay, Alaska, a high number of humpback whales were found dead in 2010. It was discovered that at least two were killed by boat collisions.

Pollution

Humpback whales, like many other creatures that live in the ocean, are at risk from **pollution**. Pollution is damage caused to water, air, or soil when harmful substances enter them.

Some types of pollution float on the water's surface.

Waste at Sea

Most of the pollution in oceans comes from land. Pipes from factories and other buildings carry waste into the sea. Rainwater washes oil, waste, and chemicals off fields into rivers that flow into the sea. Large ocean-going ships dump waste into the sea, too.

Polluted Food

Whales swallow waste in water and eat **prey** that contain pollution. There is only a small amount of pollution in the tiny animals that whales eat, but humpbacks eat so many of the animals that the pollution builds up in their bodies. This can harm the whales and reduce their ability to **breed**.

When a humpback opens its mouth wide to feed, it may swallow pollution.

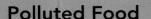

Rescue the HUMPBACK WHALE!

When you visit the beach, make sure you collect your trash and throw it away in a bin. If you leave it lying on the beach, it may wash into the sea and cause pollution.

17

Noise Disturbance

Humbacks make many different sounds. Sounds move faster through water than air, so they are a great way for whales to communicate with each other. Sadly, many human noises are disturbing whale communication.

Whale Songs

Humpback whales make more sounds than other whales, including moans, chirps, groans, and clicks. They join the sounds together to create "songs" that can last up to 30 minutes! Scientists are studying these sounds to figure out what they mean. They believe that humpbacks sing to communicate with other whales, and to call to a mate.

Whale songs travel a long way underwater.

Nuisance Noise

When people build harbors, hotels, and pipelines on shorelines, the machines they use make loud noises that travel far into the oceans. The engines and propellers of large ships and boats also make a lot of noise. This disturbs whales, and can make them move away from their feeding or breeding grounds.

Ship engines make loud noises that can harm humpback whales.

ANIMAL SOS!

Recent studies carried out on dead humpback whales in Newfoundland, Canada, discovered the animals had ear damage caused by loud sounds, such as the noise made by ship engines.

19

Climate Change

Climate change is the way the temperature of the Earth is getting warmer. It is caused partly by people burning fuels such as coal and oil. Climate change is affecting whales.

Killing Krill

Humpback whales eat lots of **krill**. Krill are small, shrimplike animals that swim in huge groups. Their numbers are declining. One reason for this is that they feed on tiny plants that grow on the underside of sea ice. Climate change is causing sea ice to melt, reducing the whales' food supply.

Adult humpback whales can eat 40 million krill in just one day.

Getting Fat

In summer, humpbacks eat 2,000 to 3,000 pounds (900–1,400 kg) of food every day! They must eat these quantities to build up fat reserves that they store in their blubber. In winter, the whales travel to breeding grounds and do not feed. Then, they live off these fat reserves. Humpbacks need lots of krill to survive.

ANIMAL SOS!

People use krill as food for farmed fish. Climate change is making sea ice melt. Fishing boats are now traveling to previously frozen areas, to catch the krill that whales rely on for their food.

Krill are only around the size of a paperclip, but humpbacks could not survive without these tiny creatures.

Whale Watching

Today, many people go whale watching in boats to see whales in the wild. People can now see how wonderful these animals are, and are trying to help them survive.

Good and Bad

When people go on whale-watching trips they appreciate how wonderful whales are, and are more likely to help them. Whale-watching trips also provide incomes for people who run the trips. However, if boats travel too close to the whales, or too many boats approach a whale at the same time, humpback feeding patterns can be disturbed.

Whale-watching trips can help whales, as long as they are carried out safely and carefully.

Bubble Netting

When a small group of whales blows bubbles as they swim around a patch of food, it is called bubble netting. The bubbles form a "net" that traps prey and forces it to the surface. There, the whales easily scoop prey into their mouths. Many tourists on whale-watching trips hope to see bubble netting.

Humpback whales catch some food by making a net of bubbles!

ANIMAL SOS!

A study in Greenland during 2007 and 2008 showed that the feeding dives of humpback whales were shorter when whale-watching boats were nearby.

Marine Reserves

Some countries, such as the United States and Australia, are creating **marine reserves** to protect whales such as the humpback.

Protecting Sea Life

Marine reserves are areas of the sea that have laws to protect the wildlife that lives there. In the Hawaii Marine Sanctuary, it is illegal to approach a humpback whale closer than 300 feet (90 m) by sea, and 1,000 feet (300 m) by air. Officers in reserves also rescue whales entangled in nets. Coastal marine reserves are very important because this is where whales give birth to young.

This sign tells visitors that they are in Makapuu Humpback Whale Sanctuary, in Hawaii.

Whale Calves

Whale babies, called calves, are born underwater and must come to the surface to breathe immediately. That is why whales give birth to young in shallow coastal waters. Mothers stay close to their calves, to feed and protect them. Newborn humpback calves can drink 100 pounds (45 kg) of their mothers' milk each day. Calves stay close to their mothers to learn skills, such as how to swim quickly.

Rescue the HUMPBACK WHALE!

Whales can live safe from harm in marine reserves.

In 2012, a huge marine reserve measuring 2,700 square miles (700,000 ha) was created. It lies off the coast of western Australia and is one of the largest areas in the world in which humpbacks give birth to their young.

Protecting Humpback Whales

Some people work in **conservation** organizations to protect the world's wonderful humpback whales. These groups make other people aware of the problems facing the whales, and raise money to help protect them in different ways.

Conservation Groups

Conservation groups that help whales include the Whale and Dolphin Conservation (WDC) and the World Wildlife Fund (WWF). These groups study humpback whales to discover the problems they face. They tell people around the world about what is happening to humpback whales. They ask for public support to persuade governments to help whales.

Greenpeace sends boats to monitor whaling ships.

Projects in Action

Conservation organizations buy equipment and pay scientists to carry out whale research. They encourage countries to set up marine reserves and safe coastal areas for whales. The organizations teach fishermen how to fish in ways that do not damage whale food supplies, and that reduce the chance of whales being caught in fishing nets.

Conservation groups work hard to protect humpback whales.

Rescue the HUMPBACK WHALE!

Join a conservation organization, such as the WDC. Through these organizations you could even pay to adopt a whale. Your money will fund the organization's work to protect humpback whales.

27

Will Humpback Whales Survive?

It is amazing to see young whales chasing and playing with each other. It is incredible to see adult whales leaping out of the water, and crashing down again with a mighty splash. How long will people be able to see these wonderful sights?

Making a Comeback

Many populations of humpback whale have increased since a law was made to stop hunting whales for profit in 1966. However, humpback whales are now at risk from new dangers. That is why scientists are studying these magnificent animals to understand how to help them survive.

Humpbacks are at risk, but many people are listening to their SOS.

Saving Humpbacks

The number of humpback whales is increasing, but only very slowly. Female whales begin to give birth only when they are 10 years old. They have just one calf every three years. Many calves are attacked by predators and do not survive. Only if people work together to stop illegal hunting, keep oceans clean, and create more marine reserves, will humpback whales survive in the future.

Hopefully, many humpback whales will feed in the world's oceans in the future.

Rescue the
HUMPBACK
WHALE!

Organize a school event such as a bake sale, toy sale, or **sponsored** walk to raise money for a humpback whale conservation organization.

Glossary

baleen (buh-LEEN) A fringe of hard material in a whale's mouth that filters food from water.

blowhole (BLOH-hohl) A nostril on the top of a whale's head.

blubber (BLUH-bur) A thick layer of fat.

breed (BREED) To produce young.

buoyancy (BOY-un-see) To float.

climate change (KLY-mut CHAYNG) The increase in temperature at Earth's surface.

conservation (kon-sur-VAY-shun) Working to protect animals and the environment.

equator (ih-KWAY-tur) An imaginary line drawn around the Earth, equally distant from both the North and the South Pole.

extinct (ik-STINGKT) No longer existing.

fin (FIN) A flap of skin that helps whales and fish to swim.

flippers (FLIH-purz) The front limbs of a whale.

hemisphere (HEH-muh-sfeer) Half of the Earth. Earth can be divided into the southern and northern hemispheres.

indigenous (in-DIH-jeh-nus) Born in or native to a place.

krill (KRIL) Small shrimplike creatures.

mammals (MA-mulz) Warm-blooded animals that give birth to live young, which are fed on milk from their mother's body. Humans and whales are mammals.

marine reserves (muh-REEN rih-ZURVZ) Areas of ocean where wildlife can live without being harmed by people.

migrate (MY-grayt) To travel to a different place to live for part of the year.

pollution (puh-LOO-shun) Substances or things that have harmful or poisonous effects if they enter water, air, or soil.

predators (PREH-duh-turz) Animals that kill other animals for food.

prey (PRAY) An animal that is hunted by another animal.

sponsored (SPON-surd) Given money or support to achieve a particular goal.

zooplankton (zoh-uh-PLANK-tun) Very tiny animals that float or swim in water.

Further Reading

Catt, Thessaly. *Migrating with Humpback Whales*. Animal Journeys. New York: PowerKids Press, 2011.

Parker, Steve. *Whales and Dolphins*. I Love Animals. New York: Windmill Books, 2011.

Portman, Michael. *Whales in Danger*. Animals at Risk. New York: Gareth Stevens Learning Library, 2011.

Websites

For web resources related to the subject of this book, go to: www.windmillbooks.com/weblinks and select this book's title.

Index